The Seasons of the Year

by Marcia S. Freeman

ROURKE CLASSROOM RESOURCES
The path to student success

Through the year we **observe** changes in nature. Plants and animals change. We change our activities, too.

These changes happen every year. To help us describe these changes, we divide the year into four seasons. We call them spring, summer, fall, and winter.

A year is the amount of time it takes our spinning planet Earth to go around the sun. During half of the journey, the **North Pole tilts** toward the sun. During the other half, the North Pole tilts away from the sun.

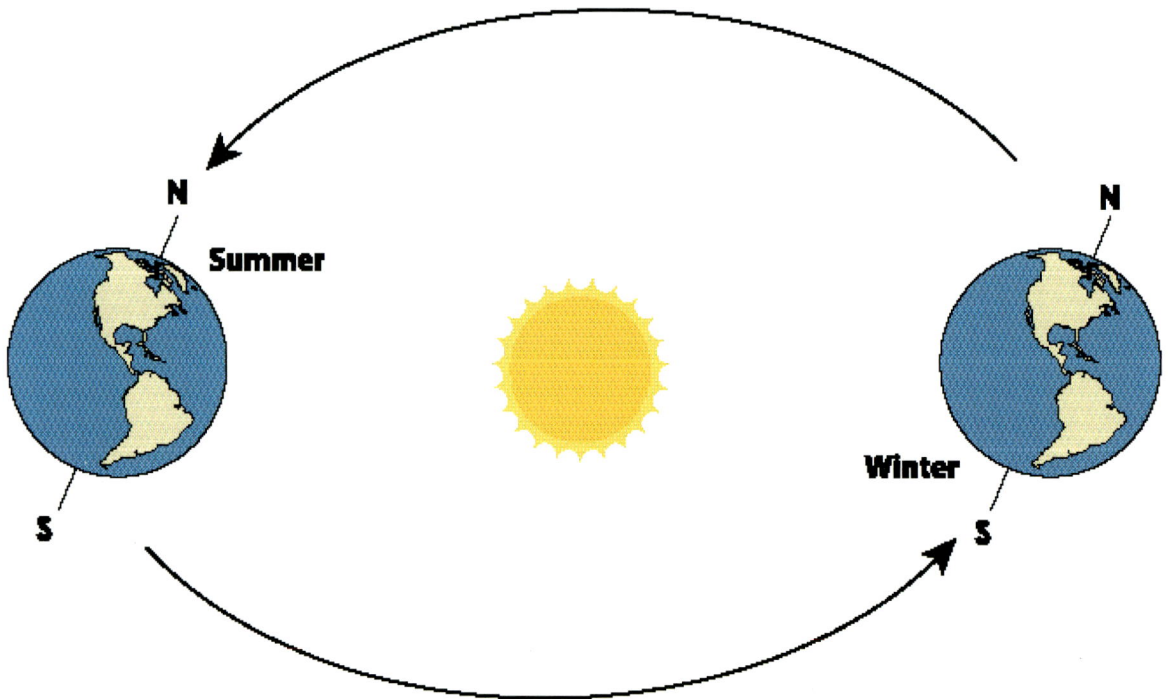

N

Summer

Winter

S

N

S

When the North Pole tilts toward the sun, we receive more of the sun's **energy** in North America. The weather gets warmer and we have summer.

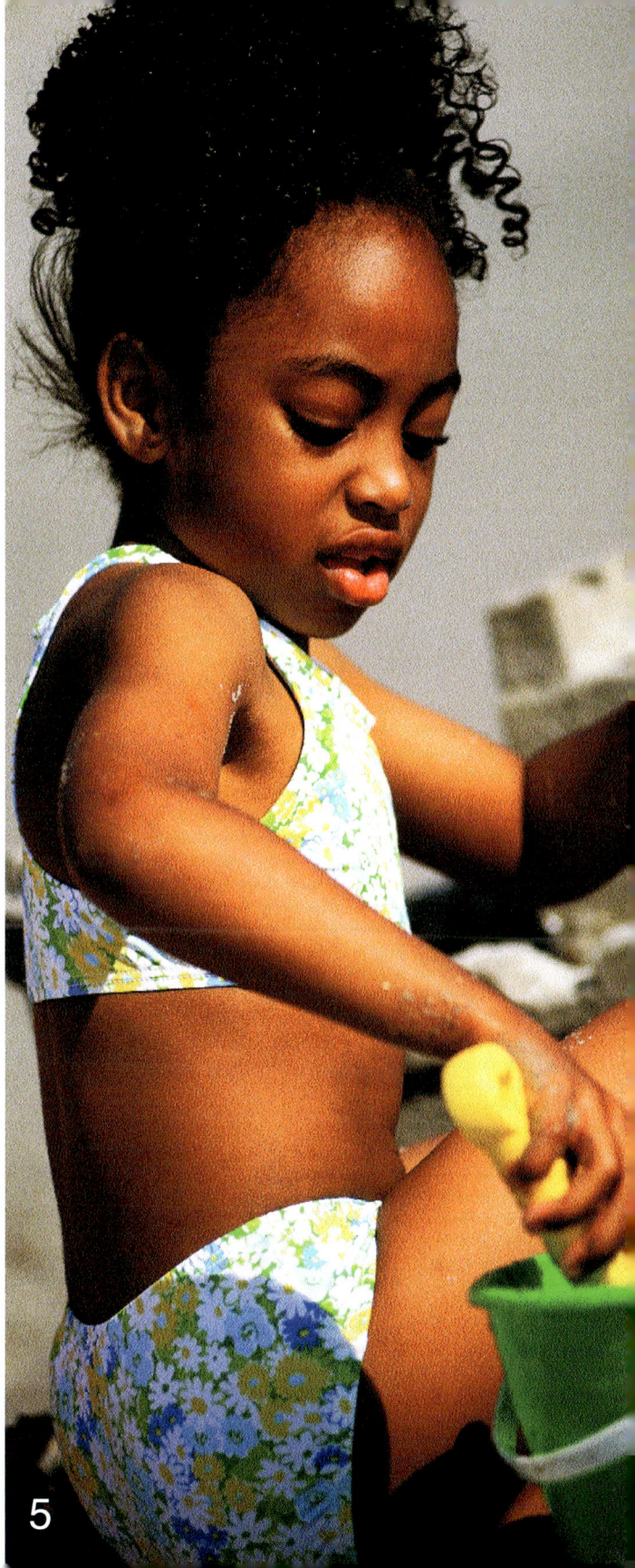

When the North Pole tilts away from the sun, we receive less of the sun's energy. The weather gets colder and we have winter.

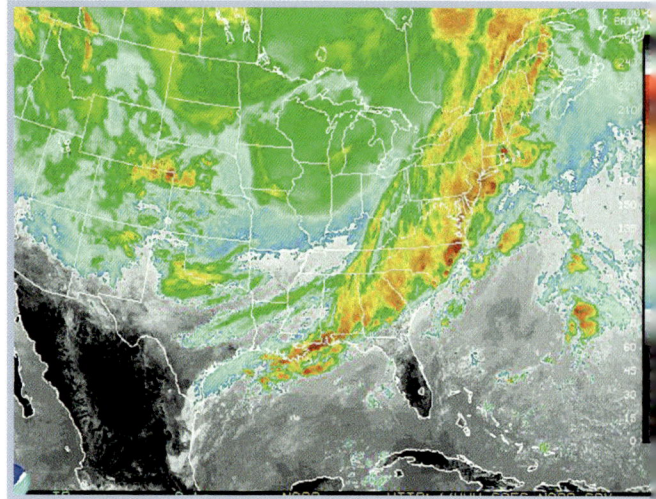

This weather map shows cold air covering most of the United States.

We notice other things change besides the temperature. For example, winter days are shorter than summer days. It may be dark when we catch the morning school bus.

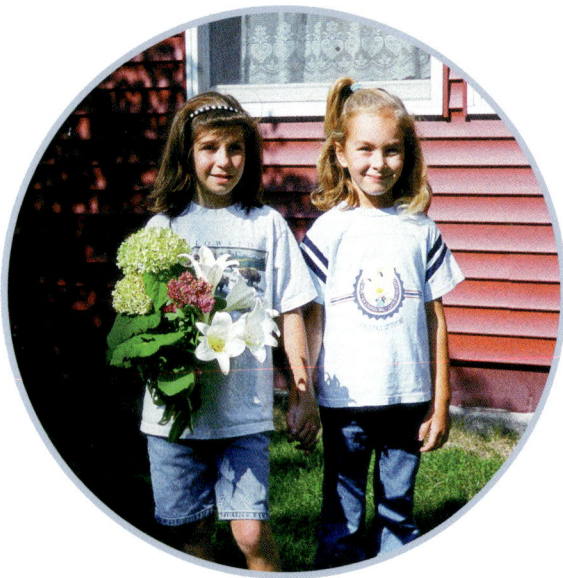

In the spring we see the grass get greener and grow. Flowers bloom and birds lay eggs.

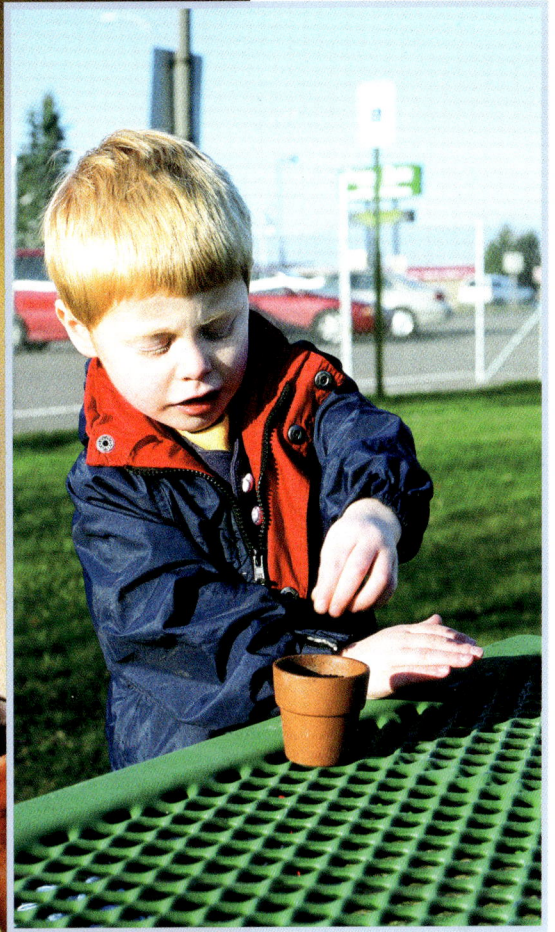

We plant seeds
and play
baseball.

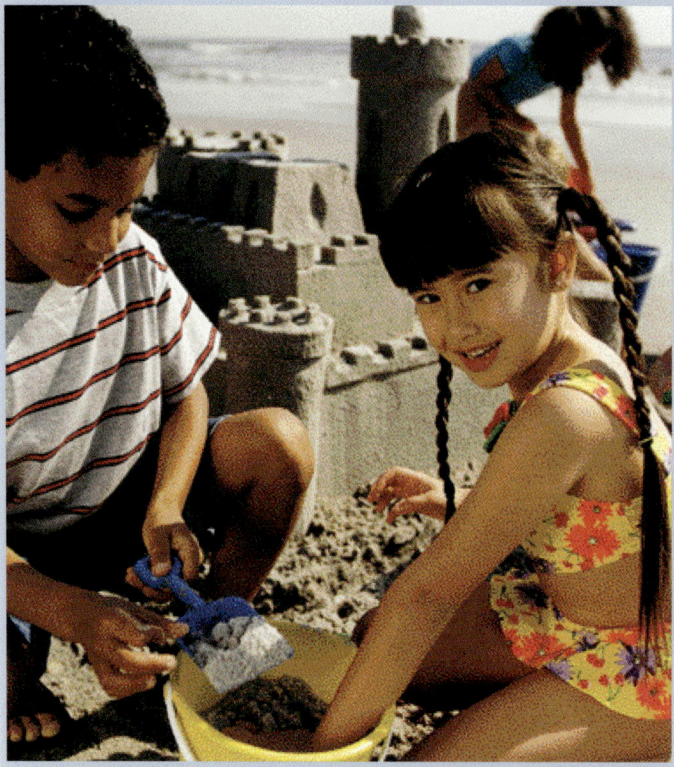

In the summer, lightning and thunderstorms bring rain. Farms **crops** grow, and families enjoy the long summer days.

In the fall, farmers **harvest** many of their crops. Children go back to school.

In the fall, animals get ready for winter. Some birds **migrate** to warmer places, and squirrels bury acorns.

These box turtles have found a place to **hibernate**.

In the winter the temperature drops. In the North, snow may fall. Animals grow longer fur. They may grow white fur to **camouflage** themselves in the snow. People may catch colds.

Sometimes we use the seasons to describe our lives. "My birthday in the spring." "It's fall, time to harvest our pumpkins." "My grandmother is going to Florida for the winter."

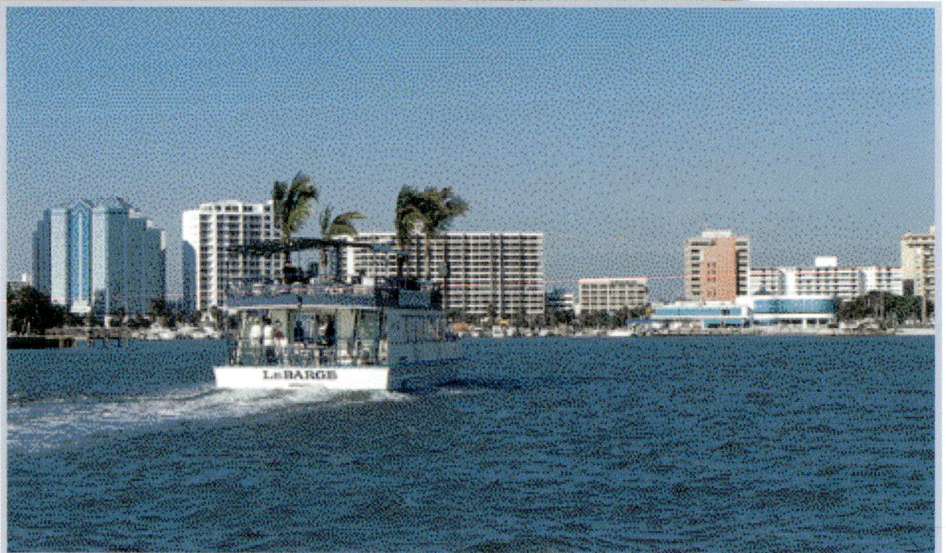

Spring, summer, fall, and winter go by every year. The passing of the seasons is just another one of nature's **cycles**.

Can you name the season for each picture?

Glossary

camouflage	make something harder to see in surroundings
crops	plants grown for food
cycles	series of repeating events
energy	heat, light
harvest	gather fruit, vegetables, or grain
hibernate	to spend the winter in a sleep-like state
observe	notice
migrate	move from one place to another with a change of season
North Pole	the northern end of the earth's axis
tilts	leans

Definitions

Index